FROZEN
Cocktails

**OVER 100 DRINKS FOR RELAXED
AND REFRESHING ENTERTAINING**

13-Digit ISBN: 978-1-60433-855-3
10-Digit ISBN: 1-60433-855-5

This book may be ordered by mail from the publisher. Please include $5.99 for postage and handling. Please support your local bookseller first!

Books published by Cider Mill Press Book Publishers are available at special discounts for bulk purchases in the United States by corporations, institutions, and other organizations. For more information, please contact the publisher.

Cider Mill Press Book Publishers
"Where good books are ready for press"
PO Box 454
12 Spring Street
Kennebunkport, Maine 04046
Visit us online!
cidermillpress.com

Typography: Bushcraft, Fenway Park JF, Helvetica Rounded, Neutraface 2 Text, Sentinel

Photo courtesy of Appleseed Press Book Publishers on page 202.
All other photos used under official license from Shutterstock.com.

Printed in China
2 3 4 5 6 7 8 9 0

FROZEN
Cocktails

OVER 100 DRINKS FOR RELAXED
AND REFRESHING ENTERTAINING

CIDER MILL PRESS

BOOK
PUBLISHERS
KENNEBUNKPORT, MAINE

Contents

Introduction

Crystal blue water. Golden sunshine. Lounge chairs by the pool. Barbecues with family and friends. A Caribbean vacation so relaxing that you finally feel in touch with the natural order of things.

The mere mention of a frozen cocktail conjures these warm, enjoyable images. With nothing more than incorporating a bit of ice, a cocktail goes from tasty to transcendent, allowing you to journey far beyond what is immediately before you.

But for some reason, most people's imaginations fail to get past the Margarita, Piña Colada, Daiquiri, and Mudslide when they think of frozen delights. And while those classics shouldn't be overlooked, there's no reason that the large shadow they cast should drown out a number of other delicious, refreshing drinks.

This book intends to give some of those other icy beverages a place in the sun. By doing nothing more than combining the wide range of flavors available in the spirits world with the fresh ingredients that the summer is famous for, these various treats will transform your view of what you are capable of whipping up in a blender.

Yes, it's an exciting prospect. But before you go and attempt to whip up a slushy version of a Dirty Martini, we recommend trying your hand at these tried-and-true recipes to get an idea of what works, and what is better left to a cocktail shaker or mixing glass.

So drag that blender out from the back of the cabinet and start filling those ice trays—it's time to transform your backyard into a summertime spot where you can refresh and impress whoever drops by.

Rum

With the Daiquiri and Piña Colada on its side, rum is the spirit that first comes to mind when people think of enjoying an icy beverage in the warm sun. Sweet and rich, it is a natural for the fruity and creamy concoctions we turn to for refreshment and relaxation.

But those standards are far from the only options rum has to offer. It is actually a very versatile spirit, able to accommodate a number of flavors. Someone looking for something that isn't so sweet should check out the Broken Compass (see page 31), while the Fernet-Branca reduction in the Pink Flamingo (see page 36) is for those skeptics who believe frozen drinks aren't for connoisseurs.

Strawberry Daiquiri

This stone-cold classic is second only to the Margarita when classic frozen cocktails are being discussed.

1 Wet the rim of your chosen glassware and dip it into the sugar.

2 Place the ice in a blender and pulse until crushed.

3 Add the remaining ingredients to the blender and puree until smooth.

4 Pour the cocktail into the rimmed glass and garnish with the additional strawberries.

For the Simple Syrup: Combine 1 cup water and 1 cup sugar in a saucepan and, while stirring, bring to a boil over medium heat. When the sugar is dissolved, remove from heat and let cool.

INGREDIENTS

Sugar, for the rim

1 cup ice

1½ oz. white rum

½ oz. orange liqueur

¼ oz. simple syrup

Juice of ½ lime

½ cup strawberries, hulled and sliced

GARNISH

1 to 2 strawberries

Pineapple Daiquiri

If you're looking to make this drink even more tropical and summery, switch out the white rum for some coconut rum.

INGREDIENTS

1 cup ice

1 tablespoon fresh lime juice

¼ cup pineapple chunks

1½ oz. white rum

½ teaspoon sugar

GARNISH

1 pineapple chunk

1 Place the ice in a blender and pulse until crushed.

2 Place the remaining ingredients in the blender and puree until smooth.

3 Pour the cocktail into your chosen glassware and garnish with the additional pineapple chunk.

Hemingway Daiquiri

Created at Havana's famous La Floridita for Papa himself, this slightly drier Daiquiri is the stuff of legend.

1 Place the ice in a blender and pulse until crushed.

2 Place the remaining ingredients in the blender and puree until smooth.

3 Pour the cocktail into your chosen glassware and garnish with the lime wedge.

INGREDIENTS

1 cup ice

1½ oz. white rum

¼ oz. Luxardo

1 oz. fresh grapefruit juice

Juice of ½ lime

1 teaspoon sugar

GARNISH

1 lime wedge

Banana Daiquiri

The aged rum and the bitters give this iteration more depth than your average, everyday Daiquiri.

INGREDIENTS

1 cup ice

2 oz. aged rum

½ banana

½ oz. simple syrup (see page 11)

½ oz. fresh lime juice

GARNISH

3 dashes of Angostura Bitters & 1 banana chip

1 Place the ice in a blender and pulse until crushed.

2 Place the remaining ingredients in the blender and puree until smooth.

3 Pour the cocktail into your chosen glassware, top with the bitters, and garnish with the banana chip.

Piña Colada

Simple, easy to prepare, and delicious: it's no accident that the Piña Colada ended up a classic.

1 Place the ice in a blender and pulse until crushed.

2 Place the remaining ingredients in the blender and puree until smooth.

3 Pour the cocktail into your chosen glassware and garnish with the pineapple chunk.

INGREDIENTS

1 cup ice

2 oz. white rum

1 oz. cream of coconut

3 oz. pineapple juice

GARNISH

1 pineapple chunk

Higher Ground

Armed with spiced rum and a touch of Campari, this break from tradition is far from sacrilegious.

INGREDIENTS

1 cup ice

2 oz. spiced rum

1½ oz. pineapple juice

2 oz. Coco Lopez cream of coconut

1 oz. Reàl Passion Fruit Puree

½ oz. Campari

GARNISH

1 orange slice

1 Place the ice in a blender and pulse until crushed.

2 Place all of the remaining ingredients in a blender and puree until smooth.

3 Pour the cocktail into your chosen glassware and garnish with the orange slice.

The Great Escape

Sweet vermouth places this drink a world away from the cocktail that inspired it—the Piña Colada—and your everyday life.

1 Place the ice in a blender and pulse until crushed.

2 Place all of the ingredients in a blender and puree until smooth.

3 Pour the cocktail into your chosen glassware and garnish with the pineapple chunk and the maraschino cherry.

Tip: If you're looking for quality sweet vermouth, Cocchi, Carpano, and Dolin are brands you can always trust.

INGREDIENTS

1 cup ice

2 oz. El Dorado Dark Rum

1 oz. pineapple juice

1 oz. Coco Lopez cream of coconut

¾ oz. sweet vermouth

GARNISH

1 pineapple chunk & 1 maraschino cherry

Passion Play

Tempering the sweetness of the rums with sour passion fruit is sure to have your taste buds swooning.

INGREDIENTS

1 cup ice

1½ oz. white rum

1½ oz. dark rum

1½ oz. Monin Passion Fruit Syrup

Juice of ½ lemon

GARNISH

1 maraschino cherry

1 Place the ice in a blender and pulse until crushed.

2 Place the remaining ingredients in the blender and puree until smooth.

3 Pour the cocktail into your chosen glassware and garnish with the maraschino cherry.

Humid Wind

The combination of coconut rum and pineapple juice is a balm for almost anything, as you'll see after downing one of these.

1 Place the ice in a blender and pulse until crushed.

2 Place the remaining ingredients in the blender and puree until smooth.

3 Pour the cocktail into your chosen glassware and garnish with the grapefruit slice.

INGREDIENTS

1 cup ice

1½ oz. coconut rum

1½ oz. pineapple juice

3 oz. grapefruit juice

GARNISH

1 grapefruit slice

Headless Horseman

Cachaça is distilled from fermented sugarcane juice. Its earthy, vegetal, and floral flavor has made it an increasingly popular spirit with leading mixologists.

INGREDIENTS

1 cup ice

1½ oz. unaged cachaça

¾ oz. orange juice

1½ oz. pumpkin syrup

½ oz. St. Elizabeth Allspice Dram

¾ oz. cinnamon syrup

1½ oz. coconut blend

¾ oz. fresh lime juice

GARNISH

1 orange twist

1 Place the ice in a blender and pulse until crushed.

2 Place the remaining ingredients in the blender and puree until smooth.

3 Pour the cocktail into your chosen glassware and garnish with the orange twist.

For the Pumpkin Syrup: Add 1 cup of pumpkin puree to a basic simple syrup (see page 11) when it is boiling. After 1 minute, remove from heat, let cool, and strain before using.

For the Cinnamon Syrup: Add 4 to 5 cinnamon sticks to a basic simple syrup (see page 11) when it is boiling. After 1 minute, remove from heat, let cool, and strain before using.

For the Coconut Blend: Combine equal parts cream of coconut and coconut milk.

Broken Compass

Crown Royal, the king of Canadian whiskies, lends its legendary smooth taste to this cocktail.

1 Place the ice in a blender and pulse until crushed.

2 Place the remaining ingredients in the blender and puree until smooth.

3 Pour the cocktail into your chosen glassware and garnish with the maraschino cherry.

INGREDIENTS

1 cup ice

1½ oz. white rum

1 oz. Crown Royal whisky

1 oz. brandy

¼ oz. grenadine

GARNISH

1 maraschino cherry

Mango Tango

Some folks will claim that it isn't a true Mango Tango unless a Strawberry Daiquiri (see page 11) is layered into the drink, but we think it is more than capable of standing on its own.

INGREDIENTS

1 cup ice

1 oz. dark rum

1 oz. coconut rum

1 oz. orange liqueur

Juice of ½ lime

½ cup mango chunks

1½ oz. pineapple juice

GARNISH

1 mango slice

1 Place the ice in a blender and pulse until crushed.

2 Place the remaining ingredients in the blender and puree until smooth.

3 Pour the cocktail into your chosen glassware and garnish with the slice of mango.

Hurricane

Warning: this cocktail is as dangerous as it is delicious. Proceed with caution.

1 Place the ice in a blender and pulse until crushed.

2 Place the remaining ingredients in the blender and puree until smooth.

3 Pour the cocktail into your chosen glassware and garnish with the orange wheel and maraschino cherry.

INGREDIENTS

1 cup ice

1½ oz. dark rum

1½ oz. white rum

1½ oz. Monin Passion Fruit Syrup

1½ oz. orange juice

1 oz. pomegranate juice

Juice of ½ lime

GARNISH

1 orange wheel & 1 maraschino cherry

Pink Flamingo

The Banks 5 Island Rum and the Fernet-Branca reduction lend this cocktail a balance and depth that is rare in any drink.

INGREDIENTS

½ cup ice

1½ oz. Banks 5 Island Rum

½ oz. Liber & Co. Pineapple Gum Syrup

1 oz. hibiscus tea, chilled

½ oz. condensed milk

½ oz. cream of coconut

Splash of Fernet–Branca reduction

1 Place the ice in a blender and pulse until crushed.

2 Place all of the remaining ingredients, except for the reduction, in a blender and puree until smooth.

3 Place the reduction in your chosen glassware and then pour the contents of the blender on top.

For the Fernet-Branca Reduction: In a saucepan, combine equal parts Fernet–Branca and sugar and cook over medium heat until the mixture has been reduced to a syrup.

Kama'aina

Rhum agricole is distilled from sugarcane juice that has not been fermented, and has acquired a cult following due to the pure, slightly grassy flavor it lends to cocktails.

1 Place the ice in a blender and pulse until crushed.

2 Place the remaining ingredients in the blender and puree until smooth.

3 Pour the cocktail into your chosen glassware and garnish with the orchid blossom.

For the #9: Combine 2 oz. Reàl Ginger Syrup with 1 oz. almond paste. Add 1 teaspoon of Alamea Pimento Liqueur and stir to combine.

INGREDIENTS

1 cup ice

1 oz. Alamea Spiced Rum

1 oz. rhum agricole

1 oz. guava nectar

½ oz. #9

½ oz. Reàl Cream of Coconut

½ oz. fresh lime juice

2 dashes of Angostura Bitters

GARNISH

1 orchid blossom

Dan's Piña Paradise

The mixture of citrus juices and the extra-special #9 mixture will have you breaking out the tiki torches.

INGREDIENTS

1 cup ice

2 oz. Bacardi Añejo Cuatro Rum

½ oz. Plantation Pineapple Rum

½ oz. fresh lime juice

½ oz. grapefruit juice

½ oz. orange juice

1 oz. #9 (see page 39)

4 fresh pineapple chunks

GARNISH

1 pineapple slice

1 Place the ice in a blender and pulse until crushed.

2 Place the remaining ingredients in the blender and puree until smooth.

3 Pour the cocktail into your chosen glassware and garnish with the pineapple slice.

Logan's Rum

Playing tart cranberry off the soft sweetness of the rums lends this concoction a pleasant, accessible depth.

1 Place the ice in a blender and pulse until crushed.

2 Place the remaining ingredients in the blender and puree until smooth.

3 Pour the cocktail into your chosen glassware and garnish with the lime wheel.

INGREDIENTS

1 cup ice

1½ oz. white rum

1½ oz. coconut rum

3 oz. cranberry juice

Dash of lime juice

GARNISH

1 lime wheel

Cat's Cradle

After tasting this one, you'll find yourself wondering if absolutely everything would be better frozen.

INGREDIENTS

1 cup ice

2 oz. coconut rum

2 oz. orange juice

2 oz. cranberry juice

Splash of triple sec

GARNISH

1 orange slice

1 Place the ice in a blender and pulse until crushed.

2 Place the remaining ingredients in the blender and puree until smooth.

3 Pour the cocktail into your chosen glassware and garnish with the orange slice.

Desert Lily

Aloe vera juice's natural sour taste and the floral notes in the lavender flower water add an exquisite roundness to this drink.

1 Place the ice in a blender and pulse until crushed.

2 Place the remaining ingredients in the blender and puree until smooth.

3 Pour the cocktail into your chosen glassware and garnish with the maraschino cherry.

INGREDIENTS

1 cup ice

2 oz. rum (Caña Brava preferred)

1 oz. aloe vera juice

¾ oz. fresh lime juice

¾ oz. simple syrup (see page 11)

¼ oz. fresh lemon juice

2 to 3 drops Fee Brothers Lavender Flower Water

GARNISH

1 maraschino cherry

The Black Madonna

While any cocktail heading in this many directions is grounds for skepticism, The Black Madonna will quickly restore your faith.

INGREDIENTS

½ cup coffee ice cubes

½ cup ice

1 oz. white rum

1 oz. coffee liqueur

1 oz. Irish cream

Dash of crème de menthe

GARNISH

1 sprig of mint

1 Place the coffee ice cubes and the ice in a blender and pulse until crushed.

2 Place the remaining ingredients in the blender and puree until smooth.

3 Pour the cocktail into your chosen glassware and garnish with the sprig of mint.

For the Coffee Ice Cubes: Simply pour 2 cups of room-temperature coffee into an ice cube tray and place in the freezer. Store coffee ice cubes in resealable plastic bags in the freezer so you'll always have some ready to go.

Buenos Días

There's no better way to keep cool during a scorcher than a Buenos Días in the morning.

1 Place the coffee ice cubes and the ice in a blender and pulse until crushed.

2 Place the remaining ingredients in the blender and puree until smooth.

3 Pour the cocktail into your chosen glassware.

INGREDIENTS

½ cup coffee ice cubes (see page 48)

½ cup ice

1½ oz. dark rum

½ cup coffee, chilled

Spoonful of sugar (optional)

Splash of Baileys Irish Cream

Tequila

Everyone seems to have an opinion on tequila, with a considerable number of folks begging off due to an unfortunate experience that took place during their youth. But it's likely that an overwhelming majority of those unpleasant encounters were the result of drinking a mixto, which refers to a tequila that is distilled from less than 100 percent blue agave.

If you stick to silver tequila, which is tenderly cared for by the *jimadors* that shepherd the agave from planting to harvest, you'll begin to see all that this spirit has to offer.

And it's more than just the Margarita. Tequila also lends its invigorating bite to cocktails like the Pepino (see page 95), a cilantro-and-cucumber cooler that will serve as a perfect lead-in to those simple, freshness-packed dinners that the summer is famed for.

Classic Margarita

As far as we're concerned, this cocktail made a quality blender a kitchen essential.

INGREDIENTS

Sea salt, for the rim

1 cup ice

2½ oz. silver tequila

1¼ oz. fresh lime juice

1 oz. simple syrup
(see page 11)

1½ oz. orange liqueur

GARNISH

1 lime wheel

1 Wet the rim of your chosen glassware and dip it into the salt.

2 Place the ice in a blender and pulse until crushed.

3 Place the remaining ingredients in the blender and puree until smooth.

4 Pour the cocktail into the rimmed glass and garnish with the lime wheel.

Coconut Margarita

Cutting the pleasant bite of aged tequila with the sweetness of coconut is a guaranteed recipe for success.

1 Wet the rim of your chosen glassware and dip it into the salt.

2 Place the ice in a blender and pulse until crushed.

3 Place the remaining ingredients in the blender and puree until smooth.

4 Pour the cocktail into the rimmed glass and garnish with the lime wheel.

For the Coconut Puree: Place ½ cup shredded coconut and 1 cup coconut milk in a blender and process until smooth.

INGREDIENTS

Sea salt, for the rim

1 cup ice

2 oz. añejo tequila

2 oz. coconut puree

1 oz. fresh lime juice

¼ oz. agave nectar

½ oz. orange liqueur

GARNISH

1 lime wheel

Kiwi Margarita

The stunning shade of green in this glorious cocktail will have everyone who opted for a different drink racked with envy.

INGREDIENTS

Sea salt, for the rim

1 cup ice

2 oz. reposado tequila

1 oz. fresh lime juice

½ cup ripe kiwi, diced

1 oz. simple syrup
(see page 11)

1 oz. orange liqueur

GARNISH

1 lime wheel or kiwi slice

1 Wet the rim of your chosen glassware and dip it into the salt.

2 Place the ice in a blender and pulse until crushed.

3 Place the remaining ingredients in the blender and puree until smooth.

4 Pour the cocktail into the rimmed glass and garnish with a lime wheel or a slice of kiwi.

The Hawaiian

Incredibly fragrant and slightly sour, passion fruit juice can be an acquired taste. Once you get there, you'll see the value of this golden cocktail.

1 Wet the rim of your chosen glassware and dip it into the salt.

2 Place the ice in a blender and pulse until crushed.

3 Place the remaining ingredients in the blender and puree until smooth.

4 Pour the cocktail into the rimmed glass and garnish with the lime wheel.

INGREDIENTS

Sea salt, for the rim

1 cup ice

2½ oz. reposado tequila

3 oz. passion fruit nectar

1 oz. fresh lime juice

½ oz. orange liqueur

½ oz. agave nectar

GARNISH

1 lime wheel

Pineapple Margarita

If you're looking for a slightly different experience, grill the pineapple before adding it to the blender. The caramelized sugar and hint of smoke will add yet another layer to an already delicious drink.

INGREDIENTS

1 tablespoon sea salt

1 tablespoon shredded coconut

1 cup ice

1½ oz. silver tequila

1 oz. mezcal

2 oz. pineapple juice

¼ cup fresh pineapple chunks

1 oz. orange liqueur

1 oz. fresh lime juice

GARNISH

1 lime wheel & 1 pineapple chunk

1 Combine the sea salt and shredded coconut in a small dish. Wet the rim of your chosen glassware and dip it into the mixture.

2 Place the ice in a blender and pulse until crushed.

3 Place the remaining ingredients in the blender and puree until smooth.

4 Pour the cocktail into the rimmed glass and garnish with the lime wheel and additional pineapple chunk.

Gravity's Rainbow

Buttery, sweet, and sour, few items possess a flavor as beguiling as tamarind. Lucky for you, that slippery nature is perfect for the bold taste of tequila.

1 Wet the rim of your chosen glassware and dip it into the salt.

2 Place the ice in a blender and pulse until crushed.

3 Place the remaining ingredients in the blender and puree until smooth.

4 Pour the cocktail into the rimmed glass and garnish with the additional pineapple chunk.

INGREDIENTS

Sea salt, for the rim

1 cup ice

2½ oz. reposado tequila

¼ cup fresh pineapple chunks

1 oz. tamarind nectar

1 oz. orange liqueur

2 oz. fresh lime juice

GARNISH

1 pineapple chunk

Little Fluffy Clouds

Picture a sunset in the American Southwest and you'll have an idea of how grand this particular alloy is.

INGREDIENTS

Sea salt, for the rim

1 cup ice

2½ oz. añejo tequila

1 oz. cream of coconut

2 tablespoons shredded coconut

1 oz. fresh lemon juice

½ oz. fresh lime juice

½ oz. agave nectar

1 oz. orange liqueur

GARNISH

1 orange twist

1 Wet the rim of your chosen glassware and dip it into the salt.

2 Place the ice in a blender and pulse until crushed.

3 Place the remaining ingredients in the blender and puree until smooth.

4 Pour the cocktail into the rimmed glass and garnish with the orange twist.

Green Goddess

The inclusion of mint provides an additional layer of refreshment in this cooling concoction.

1 Wet the rim of your chosen glassware and dip it into the salt.

2 Place the ice in a blender and pulse until crushed.

3 Place the remaining ingredients in the blender and puree until smooth.

4 Pour the cocktail into the rimmed glass and garnish with the sprig of mint.

INGREDIENTS

Sea salt, for the rim

¾ cup ice

3 oz. silver tequila

¾ cup fresh honeydew melon, diced

4 to 5 mint leaves

2 oz. fresh lime juice

1 oz. orange liqueur

GARNISH

1 sprig of mint

Rosalita Margarita

Creamy cantaloupe is the perfect stage for the sweet and anise-tinged flavor of basil to star upon.

INGREDIENTS

Sea salt, for the rim

¾ cup ice

2½ oz. reposado tequila

¾ cup fresh cantaloupe, diced

3 to 4 basil leaves

2 oz. fresh lime juice

1 oz. orange liqueur

GARNISH

1 sprig of basil & 1 cantaloupe chunk

1 Wet the rim of your chosen glassware and dip it into the salt.

2 Place the ice in a blender and pulse until crushed.

3 Place the remaining ingredients in the blender and puree until smooth.

4 Pour the cocktail into the rimmed glass and garnish with the sprig of basil and additional cantaloupe.

Watermelon-Basil Margarita

As you'll find, watermelon makes fast friends with almost any herb. If this is a little too sweet for your taste, try using mezcal in place of the tequila.

1 Wet the rim of your chosen glassware and dip it into the salt.

2 Place the ice in a blender and pulse until crushed.

3 Place the remaining ingredients in the blender and puree until smooth.

4 Pour the cocktail into the rimmed glass and garnish with the lime wheel.

INGREDIENTS

Sea salt, for the rim

1 cup ice

2½ oz. silver tequila

1½ oz. fresh lime juice

1 cup fresh watermelon, diced

3 to 4 basil leaves

1 oz. simple syrup (see page 11)

1¼ oz. orange liqueur

GARNISH

1 lime wheel

Under the Volcano

Turning to one of these at the end of a long day is certain to iron out any creases in your brow.

INGREDIENTS

¾ cup ice

1½ oz. mezcal

1 oz. silver tequila

½ cup apple juice

1 oz. fresh lemon juice

1 oz. cinnamon syrup
(see page 28)

½ oz. orange liqueur

GARNISH

1 lime wheel

1 Place the ice in a blender and pulse until crushed.

2 Place the remaining ingredients in the blender and puree until smooth.

3 Pour the cocktail into your chosen glassware and garnish with the lime wheel.

Toronha

The orange liqueur and splash of grenadine do just enough to temper the sharpness of the grapefruit juice in this citrusy fusion.

1 Place the ice in a blender and pulse until crushed.

2 Place the remaining ingredients in the blender and puree until smooth.

3 Pour the cocktail into your chosen glassware and garnish with a lime, grapefruit, or orange wheel.

INGREDIENTS

1 cup ice

2 oz. silver tequila

½ oz. orange liqueur

2 oz. grapefruit juice

Splash of orange juice

Splash of grenadine

GARNISH

1 lime, grapefruit, or orange wheel

Cold Desert

This is a frozen version of the popular Tequila Sunrise cocktail, which rose to prominence on a legendary tour the Rolling Stones made through America in the early '70s.

INGREDIENTS

1 cup ice

2 oz. tequila

Dash of fresh lemon juice

½ cup orange juice

Splash of grenadine

GARNISH

1 maraschino cherry &
1 orange slice

1 Place the ice in a blender and pulse until crushed.

2 Place the remaining ingredients in the blender and puree until smooth.

3 Pour the cocktail into your chosen glassware and garnish with the maraschino cherry and orange slice.

Lemonade in La Paz

The piney aroma of rosemary brings out the best in lemonade, tamping down the sweetness just enough for its refreshing qualities to come forth.

1 Wet the rim of your chosen glassware and dip it into the sea salt.

2 Place the ice in a blender and pulse until crushed.

3 Place the remaining ingredients in the blender and puree until smooth.

4 Pour the cocktail into the rimmed glass and garnish with the lemon wheel.

INGREDIENTS

Sea salt, for the rim

1 cup ice

Leaves from 1 sprig of rosemary

2 oz. silver tequila

½ oz. coconut rum

½ cup lemonade

GARNISH

1 lemon wheel

Midnight Oil

While this coffee-based drink will be perfectly fine in the morning, it is an ideal after-dinner drink on those nights you're going to be up a little later than usual.

INGREDIENTS

1 cup coffee ice cubes (see page 48)

1½ oz. tequila

1 oz. coffee liqueur

2 oz. coffee, chilled

Splash of Baileys Irish Cream

GARNISH

Dollop of whipped cream

1 Place the coffee ice cubes in a blender and pulse until crushed.

2 Place the remaining ingredients in the blender and puree until smooth.

3 Pour the cocktail into your chosen glassware and garnish with the dollop of whipped cream.

The Long Goodbye

It will be tempting to turn to this recipe any time you want a cocktail. But, if you can, reserve it for those picturesque evenings that come at the tail end of summer.

1 Place the ice in a blender and pulse until crushed.

2 Place the remaining ingredients in the blender and puree until smooth.

3 Pour the cocktail into your chosen glassware and garnish with the orange wheel.

INGREDIENTS

1 cup ice

1½ oz. tequila

1½ oz. Luxardo

Juice of ½ lime

3 oz. orange juice

GARNISH

1 orange wheel

Rainbow Road

The sweet pairing of kiwi and strawberry is a perfect spot for the slightly smoky taste of tequila to find a home.

INGREDIENTS

1 cup ice

1 kiwi, peeled and sliced

4 strawberries, sliced

2½ oz. silver tequila

2 oz. kiwi-strawberry juice

GARNISH

1 strawberry slice &
1 lime wheel

1 Place the ice in a blender and pulse until crushed.

2 Place the remaining ingredients in the blender and puree until smooth.

3 Pour the cocktail into your chosen glassware and garnish with the slice of strawberry and lime wheel.

Apple Tart

Don't let the name fool you—this cocktail is plenty sweet, thanks to the inclusion of apple schnapps.

1 Place the ice in a blender and pulse until crushed.

2 Place the remaining ingredients in the blender and puree until smooth.

3 Pour the cocktail into your chosen glassware and garnish with the slice of apple.

INGREDIENTS

1 cup ice

2½ oz. silver tequila

1¼ oz. apple schnapps

1¼ oz. apple juice

Juice of 1 lime

GARNISH

1 Granny Smith apple slice

Wise Blood

The level of tartness in this drink is sure to keep you on your toes.

INGREDIENTS

1 cup ice

6 mint leaves

2 oz. silver tequila

2 oz. cranberry juice

¼ cup cranberries

½ oz. lime juice

GARNISH

1 lime wedge

1 Place the ice in a blender and pulse until crushed.

2 Place the remaining ingredients in the blender and puree until smooth.

3 Pour the cocktail into your chosen glassware and garnish with the lime wedge.

Pepino

Cilantro and cucumber lend their incredible freshness to this cocktail, saving it from being just another sweet treat.

1 Place the ice in a blender and pulse until crushed.

2 Place the remaining ingredients in the blender and puree until smooth.

3 Pour into your chosen glassware and garnish with the lime wheel.

INGREDIENTS

1 cup ice

1 oz. simple syrup
(see page 11)

3 cilantro leaves

3 cucumber slices

2 oz. silver tequila

1 oz. orange liqueur

1 oz. pineapple juice

Juice of ½ lime

GARNISH

1 lime wheel

Sunday in Guaymas

Tequila and milk may sound like a noxious combination, but if you swaddle it in chocolate liqueur and vanilla ice cream, it's positively lovely.

INGREDIENTS

2 oz. silver tequila

2 oz. chocolate liqueur

2 oz. milk

2 scoops of
vanilla ice cream

GARNISH

Dusting of cocoa powder
& chocolate shavings

1 Place the ingredients in a blender and puree until smooth.

2 Pour the cocktail into your chosen glassware and garnish with the dusting of cocoa powder and chocolate shavings.

Vodka

Vodka tends to be slighted by those who are serious about spirits, as its clean flavor doesn't offer much to the refined palate. But as far as cocktails are concerned, this perceived weakness becomes an undeniable asset. That lack of a strong flavor allows the other ingredients to shine, creating opportunities to perfectly articulate the strengths of another component, and receive a payoff from chances taken on unorthodox ingredients.

You can see this in the Out on the Weekend (see page 125), where the sweet and refreshing qualities of watermelon and grapes will be at the fore of your mind, rather than drowning in a sea of booze. When produce is finally in season and readily available, isn't that exactly what you want?

Exiled to Siberia

Even the Dude could abide by this frozen version of his beloved White Russian.

INGREDIENTS

½ cup coffee ice cubes (see page 48)

½ cup ice

1½ oz. vodka

1½ oz. coffee liqueur

3 oz. heavy cream

GARNISH

Dollop of whipped cream

1 Place the coffee ice cubes and the ice in a blender and pulse until crushed.

2 Place the remaining ingredients in the blender and puree until smooth.

3 Pour the cocktail into your chosen glassware and top with the dollop of whipped cream.

Mudslide

Remember to take your time with this decadent cocktail, as it is stronger than it tastes.

1 Place the coffee ice cubes and the ice in a blender and pulse until crushed.

2 Place the remaining ingredients in the blender and puree until smooth.

3 Pour the cocktail into your chosen glassware and top with the dollop of whipped cream and chocolate syrup.

INGREDIENTS

½ cup coffee ice cubes (see page 48)

½ cup ice

1½ oz. vodka

1½ oz. coffee liqueur

1½ oz. Irish cream

1½ oz. heavy cream

GARNISH

Dollop of whipped cream & chocolate syrup

Mocha Mocha Mocha

By switching Irish cream out for chocolate liqueur, this becomes a great after-dinner drink.

INGREDIENTS

½ cup coffee ice cubes (see page 48)

½ cup ice

1¼ oz. vodka

1¼ oz. chocolate liqueur

1¼ oz. coffee liqueur

2½ oz. milk

GARNISH

Dusting of cocoa powder

1 Place the coffee ice cubes and ice in a blender and pulse until crushed.

2 Place the remaining ingredients in the blender and puree until smooth.

3 Pour the cocktail into your chosen glassware and garnish with the dusting of cocoa powder.

Creamsicle

Proof that you do not have to put away all childish things as an adult.

1 Place the ice in a blender and pulse until crushed.

2 Place the remaining ingredients in the blender and puree until smooth.

3 Pour the cocktail into your chosen glassware and garnish with the orange wheel.

INGREDIENTS

1 cup ice

2 oz. orange juice

2 oz. vodka

2 oz. heavy cream

Splash of triple sec

GARNISH

1 orange wheel

Shake 'N' Bake

Make sure you use quality strawberry vodka in this one, as some flavored vodkas carry an unpleasant, artificial taste.

INGREDIENTS

4 strawberries

1 oz. milk

1 oz. strawberry vodka

1 oz. vanilla vodka

3 scoops of strawberry sorbet

GARNISH

Dollop of whipped cream

1 Place the ingredients in a blender and puree until smooth.

2 Pour the cocktail into your chosen glassware and garnish with the dollop of whipped cream.

Capescrew

A twist on both the Cape Cod and the Screwdriver, this is sure to cut through the haze on a humid summer day.

1 Place the ice in a blender and pulse until crushed.

2 Place the remaining ingredients in the blender and puree until smooth.

3 Pour the cocktail into your chosen glassware and garnish with the orange wheel.

INGREDIENTS

1 cup ice

2 oz. vodka

Splash of triple sec

2 oz. orange juice

2 oz. cranberry juice

GARNISH

1 orange wheel

Cool Breeze

This frozen take on the classic Sea Breeze cocktail is perfect for those quiet moments spent by the grill on a summer night.

INGREDIENTS

1 cup ice

Juice of ½ lime

1½ oz. vodka

3 oz. cranberry juice

1 oz. grapefruit juice

GARNISH

1 grapefruit slice

1 Place the ice in a blender and pulse until crushed.

2 Place the remaining ingredients in the blender and puree until smooth.

3 Pour the cocktail into your chosen glassware and garnish with the slice of grapefruit.

Summer in the City

Because as anyone who's been there knows: even Death Valley feels more tolerable than a big city during the dog days of August.

1 Place the ice in a blender and pulse until crushed.

2 Place the remaining ingredients in the blender and puree until smooth.

3 Pour the cocktail into your chosen glassware and garnish with the lime wheel.

INGREDIENTS

1 cup ice

2½ oz. vodka

1½ oz. triple sec

1½ oz. cranberry juice

Juice of 1 lime wedge

GARNISH

1 lime wheel

Summer Splash

The touch of tartness added by the lime juice makes this simple cocktail a real head-turner.

INGREDIENTS

1 cup ice

2 oz. cranberry vodka

½ cup lemonade

½ oz. fresh lime juice

GARNISH

1 lemon wheel

1 Place the ice in a blender and pulse until crushed.

2 Place the remaining ingredients in the blender and puree until smooth.

3 Pour the cocktail into your chosen glassware and garnish with the lemon wheel.

Tip: You can make your own flavored vodka just as easily as you can buy it at the store, and the results will almost certainly be better. For the DIY version, place a handful of cranberries in a mason jar and muddle. Add 1 cup vodka and store in a cool, dark place for 3 days while agitating daily. Strain before using.

Red Dawn

The name is a nod to the grenadine, which will filter slowly down through the drink, as well as one of the finest films of the '80s.

1 Place the ice in a blender and pulse until crushed.

2 Place all of the remaining ingredients, except for the grenadine, in the blender and puree until smooth.

3 Pour the cocktail into your chosen glassware, top with the grenadine, and allow it to slowly filter down into the drink. Garnish with the maraschino cherry and the strip of orange peel.

INGREDIENTS

1 cup ice

2 oz. vodka

Juice of 1 lemon wedge

½ cup orange juice

Splash of grenadine

GARNISH

1 maraschino cherry &
1 strip of orange peel

Pear Pressure

The addition of vanilla vodka will help bring out the typically hidden creaminess of pears.

INGREDIENTS

1 cup ice

2 oz. vodka

1¼ oz. vanilla vodka

1½ oz. pear nectar

Juice of 1 lime wedge

GARNISH

1 pear slice

1 Place the ice in a blender and pulse until crushed.

2 Place the remaining ingredients in the blender and puree until smooth.

3 Pour the cocktail into your chosen glassware and garnish with the pear slice.

Vodka 123

Out on the Weekend

Perfect for those nights when all you need is a cold drink and Neil Young on the stereo.

1 Place the ice in a blender and pulse until crushed.

2 Place the remaining ingredients in the blender and puree until smooth.

3 Pour the cocktail into your chosen glassware and garnish with the watermelon cubes.

For the Puree: Place 4 oz. of fresh red grapes, 1 tablespoon lime juice, and a ½ cup of watermelon cubes in a blender and puree until smooth.

INGREDIENTS

1 cup ice

1½ oz. red grape-and-watermelon puree

1 teaspoon sugar

Juice of ½ lime

3 oz. vodka

1½ oz. red grape juice

GARNISH

Handful of watermelon cubes

Hairy Navel

Don't be thrown by the slightly unappetizing name—this amped-up version of the Fuzzy Navel is sure to delight.

INGREDIENTS

1 cup ice

1½ oz. vodka

1½ oz. peach schnapps

½ cup orange juice

Splash of pineapple juice

GARNISH

1 orange slice

1 Place the ice in a blender and pulse until crushed.

2 Place the remaining ingredients in the blender and puree until smooth.

3 Pour the cocktail into your chosen glassware and garnish with the orange slice.

Blue Christmas

Can't afford a trip to the tropics? No problem. This stunning blue drink will have you there in minutes.

1 Wet the rim of your chosen glassware and dip it into the coconut.

2 Place the ice in a blender and pulse until crushed.

3 Place the remaining ingredients in the blender and puree until smooth.

4 Pour the cocktail into the prepared glass and garnish with the pineapple chunk and the maraschino cherry, if desired.

INGREDIENTS

Shredded coconut, for the rim

1 cup ice

1½ oz. vodka

1½ oz. blue curaçao

½ cup lemonade

Juice of 1 lime wedge

GARNISH

1 pineapple chunk & 1 maraschino cherry (optional)

Melon Ball

Serious drinkers will be tempted to snicker at anything containing Midori, but this vibrant cocktail is the antidote to such snobbery.

INGREDIENTS

1 cup ice

1½ oz. vodka

1½ oz. Midori

½ cup pineapple juice

Juice of 1 lime wedge

GARNISH

2 to 3 melon balls

1 Place the ice in a blender and pulse until crushed.

2 Place the remaining ingredients in the blender and puree until smooth.

3 Pour into your chosen glassware and garnish with 2 to 3 melon balls.

Arnie's Army

Inject a little vodka, a few raspberries, and some ice into a classic Arnold Palmer and you'll start to understand why Arnie had some of the most fervent followers in all of sports.

1 Place the ice in a blender and pulse until crushed.

2 Place the remaining ingredients in the blender and puree until smooth.

3 Pour into your chosen glassware and garnish with the lemon wheel.

INGREDIENTS

1 cup ice

1½ oz. vodka

¼ cup frozen raspberries

2½ oz. lemonade

2½ oz. sweetened iced tea

GARNISH

1 lemon wheel

Gin

Having lent its talents to a stone-cold summer classic like the Gin & Tonic, it's easy to see why no one's asked much of gin in the frozen realm. Yet the minty flavor and numerous botanicals that make the G & T everyone's go-to once the weather warms also make gin a natural base for those who are desperate for frozen refreshment during the dog days.

The Salty Mutt (see page 141) is a good place to cut your teeth if you're wary of gin in your blender, with salt bringing the best out of both the gin and the grapefruit juice. Those who want something tropical need look no further than the Singapore Sling (see page 142), which the recent cocktail renaissance has rescued from the artificial hell the '80s had relegated it to.

Morning Becomes Electra

With toothpaste and orange juice renowned as a deadly duo, it seems like the combination of minty gin and orange liqueur would be tragic. As you'll see, it's anything but.

INGREDIENTS

1 cup ice

1½ oz. gin

½ oz. dry vermouth

½ oz. orange liqueur

2 dashes of orange bitters

GARNISH

1 orange slice or
1 sprig of mint

1 Place the ice in a blender and pulse until crushed.

2 Place the remaining ingredients in the blender and puree until smooth.

3 Pour the cocktail into your chosen glassware and garnish with an orange slice or a sprig of mint.

Salty Mutt

By salting the rim and adding cranberry juice, you'll be surprised by how pleasantly sweet this take on the Salty Dog becomes.

1 Wet the rim of your chosen glassware and dip it into the salt.

2 Place the ice in a blender and pulse until crushed.

3 Place the remaining ingredients in the blender and puree until smooth.

4 Pour the cocktail into the rimmed glass and garnish with the grapefruit wheel.

INGREDIENTS

Salt, for the rim

1 cup ice

2 oz. gin

2 oz. grapefruit juice

2 oz. cranberry juice

GARNISH

1 grapefruit wheel

Singapore Sling

Cocktail culture has revived this classic, which during the 1980s was little more than gin, bottled sour mix, and grenadine.

INGREDIENTS

1 cup ice

2 oz. gin

2 oz. cherry brandy

1 tablespoon Cointreau

2 tablespoons Bénédictine

½ oz. grenadine

2 tablespoons fresh lime juice

2 oz. pineapple juice

GARNISH

1 maraschino cherry

1 Place the ice in a blender and pulse until crushed.

2 Place the remaining ingredients in the blender and puree until smooth.

3 Pour the cocktail into your chosen glassware and garnish with the maraschino cherry.

Gin and Juice

Just one taste and you'll see why this simple combination once received an ode from a hip-hop legend.

1 Place the ice in a blender and pulse until crushed.

2 Place the remaining ingredients in the blender and puree until smooth.

3 Pour the cocktail into your chosen glassware and garnish with the lime wheel.

INGREDIENTS

1 cup ice

3 oz. gin

3 oz. cranberry juice

Splash of triple sec

Juice of ½ lime

GARNISH

1 lime wheel

Cherry Baby

Don't get ahead of yourself and think that this is going to be sweet. Luxardo, which is distilled from the pits and sour fruit of the marasca cherry, is far drier than the gleaming jars in the supermarket would have you expect.

INGREDIENTS

½ cup ice

¼ cup frozen cherries

2 oz. gin

2 oz. Luxardo

2 oz. fresh lemon juice

Splash of simple syrup (see page 11)

GARNISH

1 maraschino cherry

1 Place the ice in a blender and pulse until crushed.

2 Place the remaining ingredients in the blender and puree until smooth.

3 Pour the cocktail into your chosen glassware and garnish with the maraschino cherry.

Hand Grenade

While the title is more of a nod to pomegranate in French (*grenade*), this one goes down so easy that it can sneak up on you if you're not careful.

1 Place the ice in a blender and pulse until crushed.

2 Place the remaining ingredients in the blender and puree until smooth.

3 Pour the cocktail into your chosen glassware and garnish with the lime wheel.

INGREDIENTS

1 cup ice

6 mint leaves

3 oz. gin

3 oz. pomegranate juice

1 oz. fresh lime juice

GARNISH

1 lime wheel

Snow Globe

The foamy consistency provided by the egg white makes this drink look so good that you'll almost feel bad about consuming it.

INGREDIENTS

1 cup ice

2 oz. gin

2 oz. white chocolate liqueur

Splash of crème de menthe

1 tablespoon egg white

GARNISH

Dusting of nutmeg & 1 cinnamon stick

1 Place the ice in a blender and pulse until crushed.

2 Place the remaining ingredients in the blender and puree until smooth.

3 Pour the cocktail into your chosen glassware and garnish with the dusting of nutmeg and the cinnamon stick.

Greyhound

This drink is ideal for those days when your patience has worn a little bit thin and you just want to toss together the few things you have on hand, sit down, and relax.

1 Place the ice in a blender and pulse until crushed.

2 Place the remaining ingredients in the blender and puree until smooth.

3 Pour the cocktail into your chosen glassware and garnish with the sprig of rosemary and the grapefruit twist.

INGREDIENTS

1 cup ice

2 oz. gin

½ cup grapefruit juice

GARNISH

1 sprig of rosemary &
1 grapefruit twist

Lake Shore Drive

Few big cities ever approach the glory of Chicago in the summertime. This ultra-refreshing cocktail is an homage to that great city when it is in full swing.

INGREDIENTS

1 cup ice

2 oz. gin

1½ oz. limoncello

1 oz. simple syrup (see page 11)

1 oz. fresh lemon juice

4 to 5 mint leaves

GARNISH

2 mint leaves & 1 lemon slice

1 Place the ice in a blender and pulse until crushed.

2 Place the remaining ingredients in the blender and puree until smooth.

3 Pour the cocktail into your chosen glassware and garnish with the additional mint leaves and the slice of lemon.

The Clash

A souped-up lemonade that just may become the only drink that matters to you.

1 Place the ice in a blender and pulse until crushed.

2 Place the remaining ingredients in the blender and puree until smooth.

3 Pour the cocktail into your chosen glassware and garnish with the sprig of mint or basil.

1 cup ice

3 strawberries, hulled and sliced

2 basil leaves

2 oz. gin

½ oz. strawberry vodka

3 oz. lemonade

GARNISH

1 sprig of mint or basil

Watermelon Man

The light, citrus-forward flavor of Aperol and the sweetness of the watermelon make an ideal match for London Dry gin.

INGREDIENTS

½ cup ice

½ cup watermelon chunks, frozen

2½ oz. London Dry gin

1 oz. fresh lemon juice

¾ oz. simple syrup (see page 11)

1 oz. Aperol

1 Place the ice in a blender and pulse until crushed.

2 Place the remaining ingredients in the blender and puree until smooth.

3 Pour the cocktail into your chosen glassware.

Black Diamond Bay

This lovely fusion allows you to choose whether you just want to unplug and unwind, or marvel at the complex play of flavors.

1 Place the ice in a blender and pulse until crushed.

2 Place the remaining ingredients in the blender and puree until smooth.

3 Pour the cocktail into your chosen glassware and garnish with a lemon wheel or a lime wedge.

For the Mint Syrup: Add 6 mint leaves to a basic simple syrup (see page 11) once the sugar has dissolved. After 1 minute, remove the saucepan from heat, let cool, and strain before using.

INGREDIENTS

1 cup ice

6 frozen blackberries

1 oz. mint syrup

2 oz. gin

3 oz. lemonade

Dash of grenadine

GARNISH

1 lemon wheel or
1 lime wedge

Woolynesia

Don't get weary looking at the list of ingredients for this cocktail—the poblano and peach liqueurs will open up vistas you never even thought possible.

INGREDIENTS

1 cup ice

2½ oz. gin

1¼ oz. Ancho Reyes Verde Chile Poblano Liqueur

1 oz. fresh lime juice

¾ oz. Aperol

1 oz. passion fruit nectar

1 teaspoon ginger

1 teaspoon cinnamon

1 teaspoon Giffard Crème Pêche de Vigne liqueur

GARNISH

1 sprig of mint, 1 pineapple chunk & 1 orange slice

1 Place the ice in a blender and pulse until crushed.

2 Place the remaining ingredients in the blender and puree until smooth.

3 Pour the cocktail into your chosen glassware and garnish with the sprig of mint, pineapple chunk, and orange slice.

The Continent

Kümmel is a Dutch liqueur flavored with caraway seed, cumin, and fennel, and its unique tartness is being employed in a growing number of refreshing cocktails.

1 Place the ice in a blender and pulse until crushed.

2 Place the remaining ingredients in the blender and puree until smooth.

3 Pour the cocktail into your chosen glassware and garnish with the lemon wheel.

INGREDIENTS

1 cup ice

1 oz. Beefeater gin

¾ oz. plain, full-fat Greek yogurt

½ oz. orgeat

¾ oz. fresh lemon juice

¾ oz. aquavit

¾ oz. kümmel

GARNISH

1 lemon wheel

The Last Word

As aesthetically appealing as it is delicious, break this drink out any time you're looking to impress someone known for their discerning eye.

INGREDIENTS

1 cup ice

1 oz. gin

1 oz. Chartreuse

1 oz. Luxardo

1 oz. fresh lime juice

GARNISH

1 lime wheel

1 Place the ice in a blender and pulse until crushed.

2 Place the remaining ingredients in the blender and puree until smooth.

3 Pour the cocktail into your chosen glassware and garnish with the lime wheel.

Whiskey

When you think frozen cocktail, whiskey is not the spirit that readily comes to mind. Seen as far more serious than fun, some aficionados shudder at the thought of it even coming into contact with ice.

However, there are varieties of whiskey that thrive in the sweet space where frozen cocktails typically reside. Bourbon—thanks to the sweetness resulting from its corn-centric mash bill, and the vanilla and caramel notes stemming from being aged in charred oak barrels—is a natural fit for both creamy and fruity frozen drinks.

But it is not all about sweet, and for those arctic explorers who want something new in an icy blend, the cocktails featuring the spicy punch of rye whiskey are just what they're looking for.

Punch You in the Eye

The spicy rye gives this frozen spin on a whiskey punch a little bit of swagger.

INGREDIENTS

1 cup ice

2½ oz. rye whiskey

2½ oz. unsweetened iced tea

1½ oz. orange juice

Dash of bitters

GARNISH

1 orange slice

1 Place the ice in a blender and pulse until crushed.

2 Place the remaining ingredients in the blender and puree until smooth.

3 Pour the cocktail into your chosen glassware and garnish with the orange slice.

The Juice Is Loose

Cranberry always seems to get paired with vodka or gin, but you'll find it makes fast friends with rye whiskey.

1 Place the ice in a blender and pulse until crushed.

2 Place the remaining ingredients in the blender and puree until smooth.

3 Pour the cocktail into your chosen glassware and garnish with the maraschino cherry.

INGREDIENTS

1 cup ice

3 oz. rye whiskey

1½ oz. cranberry juice

¼ cup cranberries

Splash of simple syrup (see page 11)

Dash of aromatic bitters

GARNISH

1 maraschino cherry

A Rose for Emily

This cocktail is one of those rare moments when complexity is a boon, rather than a cause for dismissal.

INGREDIENTS

½ cup ice

¼ cup watermelon chunks, frozen

2½ oz. bourbon

1½ oz. Monin Watermelon Syrup

½ oz. Pama Pomegranate Liqueur

4 to 5 drops of Bittermens Hopped Grapefruit Bitters

½ oz. fresh lime juice

8 mint leaves

3 cucumber wheels

GARNISH

2 to 3 mint leaves

1 Place the ice in a blender and pulse until crushed.

2 Place the remaining ingredients in the blender and puree until smooth.

3 Pour the cocktail into your chosen glassware and garnish with additional mint leaves.

That's My Number

Due to an innovative aging process, Maker's 46 is smoother and oakier than most bourbons. Don't worry though, it still carries bourbon's famous hints of vanilla and caramel.

1 Place the ice in a blender and pulse until crushed.

2 Place the remaining ingredients in the blender and puree until smooth.

3 Pour the cocktail into your chosen glassware and garnish with additional pomegranate arils.

INGREDIENTS

1 cup ice

3 oz. Maker's 46 bourbon

1½ oz. pomegranate juice

¼ cup pomegranate arils

¾ oz. honey

¾ oz. fresh lemon juice

GARNISH

Pomegranate arils

Summertime Is Here

No matter how hot and humid it gets, this simple combination of bourbon, honey, and citrus juices will be there to cool you down.

INGREDIENTS

1 cup ice

3 oz. bourbon

1 oz. honey syrup

1 oz. fresh lemon juice

2 oz. grapefruit juice

Dash of Angostura Bitters

GARNISH

1 grapefruit slice

1 Place the ice in a blender and pulse until crushed.

2 Place the remaining ingredients in the blender and puree until smooth.

3 Pour the cocktail into your chosen glassware and garnish with the grapefruit slice.

For the Honey Syrup: Simply substitute honey for the sugar while preparing a basic simple syrup (see page 11).

Bitter Sweet Symphony

If you're tilting your head and wondering what orgeat is, your cocktail hours are about to improve tremendously. This sweet almond syrup is the key to a number of tropical drinks, including this lovely offering.

1 Place the ice in a blender and pulse until crushed.

2 Place the remaining ingredients in the blender and puree until smooth.

3 Pour the cocktail into your chosen glassware and garnish with the pineapple chunk.

For the Vanilla-Infused Bourbon: Place one split vanilla bean in a mason jar filled with bourbon and store in a cool, dark place for at least 3 days while agitating daily. Strain before using.

INGREDIENTS

1 cup ice

½ oz. orgeat

3 dashes of
Angostura Bitters

Oils from 1 orange peel

3 oz. vanilla-infused
bourbon

1 oz. Averna Amaro

GARNISH

1 pineapple chunk

The Lafayette

Any mandarin liqueur will work, but Mandarine Napoléon, which was created for the man himself, is where you should turn if quality is your top concern.

INGREDIENTS

1 cup ice

5 mint leaves

1½ oz. bourbon

1¼ oz. fresh lemon juice

2 oz. grapefruit juice

¾ oz. mandarin liqueur

GARNISH

1 grapefruit slice

1 Place the ice in a blender and pulse until crushed.

2 Place the remaining ingredients in the blender and puree until smooth.

3 Pour the cocktail into your chosen glassware and garnish with the slice of grapefruit.

Whiskey

Pharaoh's Dance

A quality blackberry liqueur, or crème de mure, is advised for this sweet, tart, and spicy concoction. If quality matters to you as much as it should, turn to Giffard for this and all things liqueur-related.

1 Place the ice in a blender and pulse until crushed.

2 Place the remaining ingredients in the blender and puree until smooth.

3 Pour the cocktail into your chosen glassware and garnish with the lemon wheel.

INGREDIENTS

1 cup ice

¼ cup frozen blackberries

2½ oz. rye whiskey

1½ oz. blackberry liqueur

½ oz. simple syrup (see page 11)

½ oz. fresh lemon juice

GARNISH

1 lemon wheel

Clouds in My Coffee

Unfortunately, there are times when the thermometer rules out Irish Coffee as an option. Fortunately, you now have a solution to that issue.

INGREDIENTS

½ cup coffee ice cubes (see page 48)

½ cup ice

3 oz. coffee, chilled

Dash of simple syrup (see page 11)

1½ oz. Irish whiskey

1½ oz. Irish cream

GARNISH

Dollop of whipped cream (optional)

1 Place the coffee ice cubes and the ice in a blender and pulse until crushed.

2 Place the remaining ingredients in the blender and puree until smooth.

3 Pour the cocktail into your chosen glassware and garnish with the dollop of whipped cream, if desired.

Shakedown Street

Rich with notes of vanilla and caramel, bourbon is the perfect spirit to pair with ice cream.

1 Place the ingredients in a blender and puree until smooth.

2 Pour the cocktail into your chosen glassware and garnish with the dusting of nutmeg.

INGREDIENTS

2 oz. bourbon

½ cup whole milk

½ oz. simple syrup
(see page 11)

2 scoops of vanilla
ice cream

GARNISH

Dusting of nutmeg

Ball & Biscuit

It's quite possible that the richness of the bourbon cream and chocolate fudge will send you right into a nap, so make sure the hammock is close by.

INGREDIENTS

4 scoops of vanilla ice cream

2 oz. Buffalo Trace Bourbon Cream

2 oz. chocolate fudge

GARNISH

Dollop of whipped cream, candied pecans & chocolate syrup

1 Place the ingredients in a blender and puree until smooth.

2 Pour the cocktail into your chosen glassware and garnish with the dollop of whipped cream, candied pecans, and chocolate syrup.

Off the Beaten Path

Just because a drink doesn't feature one of the five major spirits doesn't mean that it is second-rate. The Grasshopper (see page 217) is a concoction that New Orleans, a city whose cocktail heritage is known the world over, is proud to claim as its own. And you'd be hard-pressed to find a more inventive and beautiful brew than the Campari Colada (see page 213), which puts the delicious bitterness of Campari to good use.

Wine fanatics also get their time in the sun in this section, with the fruity Slush Berry (see page 205) and beautiful Goodbye Blue Monday (see page 209) more than capable of scratching that itch.

One Too Many Mornings

If you're looking to ease into the day after a long night, look no further than this concoction.

INGREDIENTS

1 cup ice

2½ oz. cherry brandy

3 oz. orange juice

1½ oz. fresh lime juice

GARNISH

1 orange slice

1 Place the ice in a blender and pulse until crushed.

2 Place the remaining ingredients in the blender and puree until smooth.

3 Pour the cocktail into your chosen glassware and garnish with the orange slice.

Snowball

Advocaat is essentially a European version of eggnog, but its custardy quality makes it perfect for a frozen treat.

1 Place the ice in a blender and pulse until crushed.

2 Place the remaining ingredients in the blender and puree until smooth.

3 Pour the cocktail into your chosen glassware and garnish with the dollop of whipped cream and the maraschino cherry.

INGREDIENTS

1 cup ice

3 oz. advocaat

½ oz. fresh lime juice

Dash of maple syrup

3 oz. lemonade

GARNISH

Dollop of whipped cream & 1 maraschino cherry

Roll Tide

When it's still warm but the crispness that fall is famous for has entered the air, the Roll Tide is exactly what you're looking for.

INGREDIENTS

1 cup ice

¾ oz. peach liqueur

¾ oz. amaretto

¾ oz. sloe gin

5 oz. orange juice

Dash of grenadine

GARNISH

1 orange slice & 1 maraschino cherry

1 Place the ice in a blender and pulse until crushed.

2 Place the remaining ingredients in the blender and puree until smooth.

3 Pour the cocktail into your chosen glassware and garnish with the orange slice and maraschino cherry.

Slush Berry

With the antioxidants from the red wine and all those berries, this is about as healthy as a frozen cocktail can get.

1 Place the ice in a blender and pulse until crushed.

2 Place the remaining ingredients in the blender and puree until smooth.

3 Pour the cocktail into your chosen glassware.

INGREDIENTS

½ cup ice

3 oz. sweet red wine

10 blueberries, frozen

5 raspberries, frozen

5 strawberries, frozen

1 oz. orange juice

2 oz. triple sec

How Bizarre

It's not often that you'll toss Champagne in the blender, but we think you'll be converted after trying this delicious take on a sparkling sangria.

INGREDIENTS

½ cup ice

3 oz. watermelon chunks, frozen

¼ oz. simple syrup (see page 11)

½ oz. kiwi, diced and frozen

3 oz. Champagne

GARNISH

1 lime wheel

1 Place the ice in a blender and pulse until crushed.

2 Place the remaining ingredients in the blender and puree until smooth.

3 Pour the cocktail into your chosen glassware and garnish with the lime wheel.

Goodbye Blue Monday

The blue curaçao ice cubes aren't just there for looks—the slight bitterness they provide is key to countering all that sweetness.

1 Place the blue curaçao ice cubes and the ice in a blender and pulse until crushed.

2 Place the remaining ingredients in the blender and puree until smooth.

3 Pour the cocktail into your chosen glassware and garnish with a lemon or lime wheel.

For the Blue Curaçao Ice Cubes: Fill an ice cube tray with 2 cups of blue curaçao and freeze until solid.

INGREDIENTS

½ cup blue curaçao ice cubes

½ cup ice

3 oz. sweet white wine

2 oz. lemonade

1 oz. fresh strawberries

½ oz. dark rum

GARNISH

1 lemon or lime wheel

Thunderstruck

Your taste buds will be stunned when this rollercoaster of a cocktail is through with them.

INGREDIENTS

½ cup ice

½ cup dry white wine

1 oz. pineapple, diced and frozen

2 to 3 jalapeño pepper slices

1 oz. lemonade

½ oz. fresh lime juice

GARNISH

1 lime wheel

1 Place the ice in a blender and pulse until crushed.

2 Place the remaining ingredients in the blender and puree until smooth.

3 Pour the cocktail into your chosen glassware and garnish with the lime wheel.

Campari Colada

Campari's bitter taste has made it a divisive spirit, but when it's paired with pineapple juice and cream of coconut, even the haters can get onboard.

1 Place the ice in a blender and pulse until crushed.

2 Place the remaining ingredients in the blender and puree until smooth.

3 Pour the cocktail into your chosen glassware and garnish with the orange slice.

INGREDIENTS

1 cup ice

2 oz. Campari

3 oz. pineapple juice

1 oz. cream of coconut

1 oz. heavy cream

GARNISH

1 orange slice

The Dauphin

This exquisite combination of sweet, creamy, and spicy will have you convinced that this emulsion is descended from royalty.

INGREDIENTS

1 cup ice

2 dashes of Miracle Mile Bitters Co. Chocolate Chili Bitters

½ oz. demerara syrup

½ oz. Ancho Reyes

1½ oz. absinthe

1¼ oz. toasted coconut almond milk

GARNISH

1 star anise pod

1 Place the ice in a blender and pulse until crushed.

2 Place the remaining ingredients in the blender and puree until smooth.

3 Pour the cocktail into your chosen glassware and garnish with the star anise pod.

For the Demerara Syrup: Substitute demerara sugar for the sugar in a basic simple syrup (see page 11).

Grasshopper

Make sure you don't skimp on the ice cream for this cocktail, as this New Orleans native deserves the very best.

1 Place the ingredients in a blender and puree until smooth.

2 Pour the cocktail into your chosen glassware and garnish with the dollop of whipped cream and sprig of mint.

INGREDIENTS

2 oz. green
crème de menthe

2 oz. Bols Crème
de Cacao White

2 oz. heavy cream

2 scoops of vanilla ice cream

GARNISH

Dollop of whipped cream &
1 sprig of mint

After Five

For those times when you need the comfort of something sweet after a long day at the office.

INGREDIENTS

2 oz. coffee liqueur

2 oz. Baileys Irish Cream

2 oz. peppermint schnapps

2 scoops of vanilla ice cream

GARNISH

Miniature chocolate chips (optional)

1 Place the ingredients in a blender and puree until smooth.

2 Pour the cocktail into your chosen glassware and garnish with the miniature chocolate chips, if desired.

Mocktails

Those who decide to abstain from drinking alcohol shouldn't be stuck on the sidelines at a party, left to choose between water, seltzer, and soda while everyone else gets to quaff delicious, carefully crafted cocktails. This is particularly true during the summer, when the good vibes ushered in by the warm sun should be spread as far as possible.

If you'd like to make those folks feel as though they are seen, or you just feel like taking it easy, whip up a batch of any of the nonalcoholic options collected in this chapter.

Virgin Margarita

Simple, refreshing, and delicious, just like the cocktail it descends from.

INGREDIENTS

Sea salt, for the rim

1 cup ice

1 oz. fresh lemon juice

1 oz. fresh lime juice

1 oz. orange juice

1 oz. simple syrup
(see page 11)

GARNISH

1 lime wheel

1 Wet the rim of your chosen glassware and dip it into the salt.

2 Place the ice in a blender and pulse until crushed.

3 Place the remaining ingredients in the blender and puree until smooth.

4 Pour the drink into the rimmed glass and garnish with the lime wheel.

Virgin Strawberry Daiquiri

This is a return to childhood, when going out to dinner still seemed like something special.

1 Place the ice in a blender and pulse until crushed.

2 Place the remaining ingredients in the blender and puree until smooth.

3 Pour the drink into your chosen glassware and garnish with additional strawberries.

INGREDIENTS

1 cup ice

1 oz. fresh lemon juice

1 oz. fresh lime juice

½ oz. orange juice

¼ oz. simple syrup (see page 11)

Juice of ½ lime

½ cup strawberries, hulled

GARNISH

1 to 2 strawberries

Virgin Piña Colada

The pairing of coconut and pineapple is intoxicating even without the alcohol.

INGREDIENTS

¾ cup ice

1½ oz. cream of coconut

4½ oz. pineapple juice

GARNISH

1 pineapple chunk

1 Place the ice in a blender and pulse until crushed.

2 Place the remaining ingredients in the blender and puree until smooth.

3 Pour the drink into your chosen glassware and garnish with the pineapple chunk.

Fuzzless Navel

Peach nectar sounds like something that has descended from on high. And though it is nothing more than peach juice made with the pulp, its velvety sweetness makes that divine origin seem more than reasonable.

1 Place the ice in a blender and pulse until crushed.

2 Place the remaining ingredients in the blender and puree until smooth.

3 Pour the drink into your chosen glassware and garnish with the orange slice and the maraschino cherry.

INGREDIENTS

1 cup ice

1½ oz. peach nectar

4½ oz. orange juice

GARNISH

1 orange slice & 1 maraschino cherry

Virgin Mudslide

After tasting what it does to this drink, Monin Amaretto Syrup will become a staple of your milkshakes.

INGREDIENTS

½ cup ice

1 oz. heavy cream

2 to 3 scoops of vanilla ice cream

Dash of Monin Amaretto Syrup

Chocolate syrup, to taste

GARNISH

Chocolate shavings & 1 maraschino cherry

1 Place the ice in a blender and pulse until crushed.

2 Place the cream, ice cream, and amaretto syrup in the blender and puree until smooth.

3 Coat the inside of a cocktail glass with the chocolate syrup. Pour the drink into the glass and garnish with the chocolate shavings and the maraschino cherry.

Watermelon in Easter Hay

The pinch of salt is the key here, as it draws out the sweetness of the watermelon and allows it to stand up to the strong flavor of the lime juice.

1 Place the ice in a blender and pulse until crushed.

2 Place the remaining ingredients in the blender and puree until smooth.

3 Pour the drink into your chosen glassware and garnish with the lime wheel.

INGREDIENTS

1 cup ice

½ oz. simple syrup
(see page 11)

1½ cups watermelon
chunks

Juice of 1 lime

Pinch of salt

GARNISH

1 lime wheel

Cucumber-Melon Slush

Light and lovely, this simple blend is ideal alongside the heavy dishes that make for a memorable barbecue.

INGREDIENTS

1 cup ice

½ cucumber, diced

2 golden honeydew melon slices, rind removed

1 oz. fresh lemon juice

GARNISH

1 sprig of mint

1 Place the ice in a blender and pulse until crushed.

2 Place the remaining ingredients in the blender and puree until smooth.

3 Pour the drink into your chosen glassware and garnish with the sprig of mint.

Calexico

Introducing sweet and creamy coconut into the tried-and-true partnership of lemonade and rosemary is the rare instance where messing with a good thing pays off.

1 Place the ice in a blender and pulse until crushed.

2 Place the remaining ingredients in the blender and puree until smooth.

3 Pour the drink into your chosen glassware and garnish with the lemon wheel.

For the Coconut Syrup: Add ½ cup shredded sweetened coconut to a basic simple syrup (see page 11) once the sugar is dissolved. After 1 minute, remove from heat, let cool, and strain before using.

INGREDIENTS

1 cup ice

5 oz. lemonade

1 oz. coconut syrup

Splash of agave nectar

Leaves from 1 sprig of rosemary

GARNISH

1 lemon wheel

Balearic Incarnation

Located off the coast of Spain, the Balearic Islands are where the members of Europe's glitterati go to enjoy themselves.

INGREDIENTS

Sea salt, for the rim

1 cup ice

3 oz. lemon-lime seltzer

3 oz. passion fruit nectar

1 oz. fresh lime juice

½ oz. orange juice

½ oz. agave nectar

GARNISH

1 lime wheel

1 Wet the rim of your chosen glassware and dip it into the salt.

2 Place the ice in a blender and pulse until crushed.

3 Place the remaining ingredients in the blender and puree until smooth.

4 Pour the drink into the rimmed glass and garnish with the lime wheel.

Too Matcha

A bit of spice may seem strange when you're seeking the refreshment only a frozen beverage can provide, but the jalapeño and ginger will have you rethinking that stance.

1 Place the tea ice cubes in a blender and pulse until crushed.

2 Place the remaining ingredients in the blender and puree until smooth.

3 Pour the drink into your chosen glassware and garnish with the additional slices of jalapeño.

For the Tea Ice Cubes: Combine 1 cup of ginger tea and 1 cup of green tea. Pour the mixture into an ice cube tray and freeze until solid.

INGREDIENTS

½ cup tea ice cubes

1¼ teaspoons matcha powder

½-inch piece of jalapeño pepper

1 oz. fresh lime juice

2 oz. freshly brewed ginger tea, chilled

3 oz. freshly brewed green tea, chilled

½ oz. simple syrup (see page 11)

½ oz. orange juice

GARNISH

2 to 3 jalapeño slices

Go for the Green

When you think of kiwi, your mind probably goes right to its furry skin. But this hirsute fruit is also a health powerhouse, loaded with Vitamins A, C, and B6, as well as fiber and antioxidants.

INGREDIENTS

1 cup ice

3 oz. apple juice

1½ oz. fresh lime juice

½ cup kiwi, peeled and diced

1 oz. simple syrup (see page 11)

1½ oz. orange juice

GARNISH

1 kiwi slice

1 Place the ice in a blender and pulse until crushed.

2 Place the remaining ingredients in the blender and puree until smooth.

3 Pour into your chosen glassware and garnish with the slice of kiwi.

Derby Day

Sure, the Kentucky Derby is legendary for being decadent and depraved. But someone has to keep their wits about them.

1 Wet the rim of your chosen glassware and dip it into the sea salt.

2 Place the ice in a blender and pulse until crushed.

3 Place the remaining ingredients in the blender and puree until smooth.

4 Pour into the rimmed glass and garnish with the lime wheel.

INGREDIENTS

Sea salt, for the rim

1 cup ice

2 to 3 mint leaves, plus more for garnish

1 tablespoon cucumber, diced

2 oz. fresh lime juice

2 oz. mint syrup (see page 161)

2 oz. tonic water

GARNISH

1 lime wheel

Mambo Sun

Even spicy chili powder can't stop mango's ability to enhance whatever it touches.

INGREDIENTS

½ cup ice

1 teaspoon chili powder

3 oz. mango chunks, frozen

2 oz. orange juice

2 oz. fresh lime juice

GARNISH

1 lime wheel (optional)

1 Place the ice in a blender and pulse until crushed.

2 Place the remaining ingredients in the blender and puree until smooth.

3 Pour into your chosen glassware and garnish with the lime wheel, if desired.

Index

ABOUT CIDER MILL PRESS BOOK PUBLISHERS

Good ideas ripen with time. From seed to harvest, Cider Mill Press brings fine reading, information, and entertainment together between the covers of its creatively crafted books. Our Cider Mill bears fruit twice a year, publishing a new crop of titles each spring and fall.

"Where Good Books Are Ready for Press"

VISIT US ONLINE:
www.cidermillpress.com

OR WRITE TO US AT
PO Box 454
12 Spring St.
Kennebunkport, Maine 04046